Céilís, Jigs
and Ballads

C000145549

Irish Music
In Liverpool

Kevin McManus

© Institute of Popular Music
University of Liverpool
Post Office Box 147
Liverpool L69 3BX

First published in Great Britain in 1994

ISBN 1 898806 01 2

CONTENTS

Foreword

Acknowledgment

The Roots of Irishness 1

Liverpool and the Irish 3

The Second Wave 7

Irish Traditional Music 13

The Liverpool Céilí Band and Comhaltas 15

Tunes and Pints: Liverpool Sessions 23

Old Songs in New Pubs 31

Liverpool - The Capital of Ireland? 37

Cover photo of Cream of the Barley by Derek Massey.

FOREWORD

The Liverpool Sound Series documents some of the many different traditions, practices and styles that comprise Liverpool's rich and diverse musical heritage.

The series is based on a three-year oral history project conducted by researchers from the Institute of Popular Music at the Univerity of Liverpool. The research was made possible by a grant from the Leverhulme Trust, and we would like to thank the Trust for its generous support.

Sarah Cohen
Research Fellow
Institute of Popular Music

ACKNOWLEDGMENT

The information for this book was gathered mainly by means of interviews with local musicians and members of the Irish community in the city. Thanks are due to everyone who participated.

While I have tried to be as comprehensive as possible, it was simply impractical to attempt to interview, or even mention, the vast number of people associated with the Irish music scene in Liverpool over the last forty years or so. The stories told here are just a sample.

Special thanks are due to Tommy Walsh, Sean McNamara, Mary McAndrew, Greg Quiery, Stan Ambrose, Rachel Bury, and Liam Greenslade of Liverpool University's Institute of Irish Studies, as well as my colleagues on the Leverhulme Research Team at the Institute of Popular Music.

I have attempted to corroborate oral evidence as much as possible, but when people are relying on memories of events which took place up to fifty years ago some inaccuracies are bound to slip in. Hopefully these are few and will be overshadowed by fond memories provoked by these stories about the Irish community, and their music, in Liverpool.

Kevin McManus

I think Irish music is a part of me that couldn't be expressed in any other way. I think there's an emotional and spiritual fulfilment that comes from it. I suppose it's something to do with being Irish...[1]

Liverpool, long renowned for its Irishness, was at one time referred to, on both sides of the Irish Sea, as "the capital of Ireland."

This book is about Irish music in Liverpool, but to put this in context we need to look briefly at the history of the Irish people in the city, particularly the mass emigration of the 1840s which determined the Irish nature of Liverpool. Also important is an examination of Irish organisations in the city during the Twentieth Century.

Frank Neal, in his work on sectarian violence in the city, used the term "Irish community" to mean "both the Irish-born people of Liverpool and the English-born children of Irish parents brought up in Irish communities in the town and absorbing the outlook and attitudes of the Irish."[2] In this book the definition is extended to include second and third generation descendents.

Irish districts in Liverpool retained a separate identity even when a majority of the inhabitants were locally born. Irish nationalism, Irish culture, and the Catholic faith remained strong in these communities, and second- or third-generation Irish often retained the attitudes and traditions of their Irish parents or grandparents.

The Irish Protestant community of Liverpool have their own organisations and musical culture and they use music to express their identity just as the Irish Catholic community do. Most notable here are the concertina bands, which are the marching bands of the Orange Order.

This book will attempt to throw some light on this question of Irish identity and the role that music plays in its expression.

A group photograph from a Liverpool Gaelic League Céilí (probably at The State Ballroom) in the early 1930s.

By 1821 there were 12,000 Irish people living in Liverpool, but it was not until the Great Famine of the late 1840s devastated the lives of the rural population of Ireland that the influx of Irish to the city attained epic proportions.

Neal estimates that 296,231 Irish landed in Liverpool in 1847 and over the next seven years the flow of immigrants into the city was probably of the order of half a million.³ Of those who entered Liverpool in 1847, 130,000 emigrated to the United States, others moved to the textile towns of Lancashire and Yorkshire, leaving a substantial percentage to be fed, housed and employed in Liverpool.

So by 1851 there were 83,813 Irish-born enumerated in the city's records (22% of the total population), and by 1871, after the main phase of migration had passed, there were still 76,761 Irish-born in the city (15.6% of the total).

The immigrants who came to various towns and cities in England tended to cluster together in areas which are sometimes referred to as "Little Irelands." In Liverpool, these areas were situated near the docks, to the north and south of the town centre, with a major cluster stretching from the centre outwards through Exchange, Vauxhall and Scotland wards. These "Irish" districts were characterised by large numbers of unskilled workers living in poor housing near their place of work and supported by social centres such as Irish pubs and Catholic churches. (In 1847, there were only three or four Catholic churches in Liverpool. Between 1840 and 1880 the Irish community built around another forty.)

The arrival of the Irish on such a scale inevitably caused tensions in the host city, which were exacerbated by the general economic depression of this period and the resulting overcrowding, disease, and uncertainty over employment. A large pool of cheap, mainly unskilled Irish labour was understandably regarded as undesirable by the local population.

G. Davis, in *The Irish in Britain*, has said: "The image of the Irish in the ghetto exerted a powerful influence fuelling both English prejudice and an

A Liverpool céilí from the early 1950s, probably at S.F.X. Those playing include Sean McNamara and Eamon Coyne.

Irish sense of injustice. That influence remains a dominant force in shaping modern attitudes on both sides of the Irish Sea."[4]

High death rates and epidemic disease were associated with Irish districts in Liverpool by Dr. Duncan, the city's Medical Officer of Health during that period. In the absence of medical knowledge about typhus, the Irish proved a handy scapegoat for hard-pressed authorities anxious to allay the fears of the middle classes.

According to Davis: "Specific charges were made that assumed a moral weakness in the Irish character. They arrived carrying 'Irish fever' or with dysentery. They lived in abject squalor, the result of disgusting habits....It was only a small step from these accusations, legitimised by local authorities and clergy, to full blooded racial and religious condemnation."[5]

It is hardly surprising then that prejudice against both the Irish and their offspring coloured the political life of Liverpool well into the Twentieth Century.

In 1834, William Parlour, Superintendent of the Liverpool Police, made it clear how those in authority viewed the Irish:

"...they are less cleanly in their habits, more addicted to drink, and the women less industrious."[6]

As has been the case with many immigrant groups, the Irish in Liverpool were accused of accounting for a disproportionate number of the city's crimes. Furthermore, the fact that the law breakers were perceived as being Catholic provided grist to the mill of the Protestant extremists.

Until the 1830s, Manchester rather than Liverpool had been the power base of the anti-Catholic Orange Order, dedicated to upholding the British Protestant constitution. But in response to the large Irish presence in the city in the 1840s, Liverpool became the more fertile ground for Orangeism. Of the 34 officials who attended the Grand Lodge of the Institution held in 1860, 28 were from Liverpool.

By the end of the 1840s, any sympathy there may have been for the destitute Irish had all but disappeared. The anti-Irish feeling expressed itself largely through increased sectarian bitterness.

The 1850s witnessed the establishment of 12th July, the Irish Protestant holiday, as a holiday celebration in the working class Protestant calendar in Liverpool, with 29,000 estimated to be following the procession in 1859.

Though Orange Lodges flourished in the rest of Lancashire, what gave Liverpool Orangeism its encouragement absent in other towns was the presence of what Neal terms "the baleful shadow of Ireland, which always lay across Liverpool."[7]

It is hardly surprising that sectarian tension spilled over into the streets, and there were many violent sectarian clashes in the city from the 1840s well into the next century.

Pat O'Mara, writing in 1934 about his childhood in Liverpool at the turn of the century, remembered how the city was divided along religious lines:

"The Catholic elements have their stronghold in Scotland Road along with goodly segments of the Southern end of the Dock Road. In the South the Protestants have Clive Street and Jerry Hill, and in North Netherfield Road and Lodge Lane scattered bits grouped under the name of the Orange River. The religious issue is sharply defined and anyone foolhardy enough not to heed it gets scant sympathy when trouble ensues."[8]

5

O'Mara grew up being what he terms 'Irishised' at home, learning a hatred for England at school, and he says: "What is true of me is true certainly of most slummy Irish-Catholic Britishers."[9]

Pat Ayers, writing about life in Athol Street in the North End of Liverpool between the wars, confirms this.

"A lot of the people who lived in the district were either themselves Irish, or of Irish descent. For some of these, their Roman Catholicism was allied to nationalistic fervour and political sympathy with the Irish cause."[10]

The Orange Institution still flourishes in Liverpool but with the breaking up of the tightly knit communities of old, sectarian conflict has all but disappeared.

PROGRAMME

of

Grand Irish Concert

on

St. Patrick's Eve

at the

PICTON HALL

Friday, 16th March, 1951

PRICE — Threepence

The large Irish community in Liverpool eventually set up its own organisations and a meeting held in 1929 provides the first evidence that a musical society was one of these. Held in Scotland Road, the meeting's aim was to dissolve the Council of Irish National Societies, then composed of five organisations: the Gaelic League, Sinn Fein, the Irish Self Determination League, the Irish Musical Society of Liverpool, and the Irish Foresters. (Only the Foresters and the Gaelic League turned up at the meeting so it would be fair to assume that the others had already withered.)

The end of the 1940s brought a new wave of Irish immigration to Liverpool as in the aftermath of the war Britain was rebuilding its economy and needed workers. The only active Irish organisations at this time were the GAA, the Irish Playgoers, and the Gaelic League, which had three branches—the Sean O'Donovan branch in Wood Street, the John Mitchel branch in Eldon Street, and the Four Masters branch at St. Peter and Paul's in Crosby.

There were also a couple of commercially owned venues providing music and dancing for the Irish community, most notably Lawler's on St Anne Street, run by Pat Lawler, and another club in Islington, run by his wife. From the late 1940s up until about 1964, the Shamrock Club on Lime Street, run by Eddie O'Reilly (now chair of the "Over Sixties Club" at the Irish Centre) ran weekend céilís and dances that were very popular with the young people of the Irish community. The club did not sell alcohol and local musician Sean McNamara remembers his sisters telling him how annoyed they would be when the women were left alone while the young men went off to get a drink at a nearby pub.

Of course a great many of the clergy in Liverpool during this period were Irish and more than willing to hold céilís in their parish clubs. McNamara remembers being able to go to four or five céilís a week during the 1930s and '40s. The Irish Playgoers ran annual céilís at The State Ballroom in Dale Street, and The Gaelic League in Wood Street ran weekly dances (strictly céilí dancing only).

Liverpool-born Tommy Walsh, one of the founders of the Irish Centre, sums up the changes wrought by this second major influx to Liverpool of

The Liverpool Céilí Band on stage in Ireland in 1960.

Irish emigrants, who were better equipped to assimilate than their illiterate and famished forebears:

"So we have this situation (before the influx) where there was a small active Irish community, mainly Gaelic League, living very much in a Celtic twilight, with Irish language and Irish dancing. They wouldn't allow any non-Irish dancing, would not even allow an old-time waltz. Then the Irish-born flooded in and they thought we were mad, speaking Irish and doing Gaelic dancing."

By 1948, with the second Irish influx well underway, an organisation called The Irish Association of Merseyside was formed, which was the first organisation since the Council of Irish National Societies to attempt to pull all the Irish groups together. Groups represented included the Irish National Foresters, the Gaelic League, the GAA, and the Anti-Partition of Ireland League.

The Gaelic League, however, soon went into decline and Tommy Walsh believes that ironically, the influx of Irish-born caused its demise.

"(The Gaelic League) couldn't understand how the Irish coming from

Ireland did dancing other than sixteen-hand reels, 'stack of barley' and all that. They couldn't understand it and couldn't understand why they weren't trying to speak Irish all the time. Whereas the Irish coming from Ireland had never seen céilí dancing."

"Most of my Irish friends at the time here told me that the first céilí dancing they saw was in Liverpool, and in some cases they had never heard the Irish language until they came to Liverpool."

When the Gaelic League lost its premises in Wood Street it was the beginning of the end. The League still ran céilís on a Sunday night in various venues, but the language classes ceased. It became obvious during the late 1950s and early 1960s that the Irish community, which was now very large, had outgrown the Gaelic League. The community's needs had become more than Irish language classes and céilí dancing.

One group of people believed Liverpool's Irish required an Irish centre which would cater for all the community's needs. In 1961 the Irish Centre Building Fund was started. Led by a small group of dedicated people, the project was a success. In December 1964, the premises on Mount Pleasant were opened informally, with the formal opening taking place on 1 February, 1965. By the end of the first year there were 1,635 members.

Within weeks of the opening Maírin Bolger had started an Irish dancing class at the Centre, which is still operating under her tutelage today.

By 1973 the scale of activities were so great that they had outgrown the premises and an extension was opened.

The onset of 'the Troubles' in Northern Ireland in the late 1960s undoubtedly affected the Irish community in Liverpool, particularly when issues such as the H Block Campaign and the Hunger Strikes came to the fore. It was a period when, as Tommy Walsh puts it, "Nobody in this country wanted to know the Irish community,". It was also a period when a large group of people began to realise their "Irishness" for the first time.

There are a number of reasons for the recent reawakening of young people's interest in their Irish identity. Bands like The Pogues in the 1980s made Irish music that was exciting and relevant to second and third generation Irish youngsters in Britain. The Catholic religion, which was traditionally the way Irish emigrants expressed their identity, went into decline, particularly with young people, so other means of expressing this identity were explored. The hostility towards certain aspects of Irish culture (which was a result of the long history of sectarian conflict discussed earlier) became less pronounced as sectarianism in Liverpool declined.

One concrete example of this increased interest in all things Irish are the numbers taking Irish language classes in the city. A new evening class which began at the University of Liverpool in 1992 attracted over 60 students, while Tony Birtles, who teaches two night school classes, has another twenty-odd students.

Today the Irish Centre is as important as ever to the local Irish community. There is probably no better opportunity to witness this than on a Sunday lunchtime when the building is a hive of activity and filled with people of all ages. Irish papers are sold in the shop and provide topics of conversation, an Irish band plays in the main hall, while Comhaltas have their classes for teaching young people Irish music. There is also an Irish language class for children.

Tommy Walsh gives one small example of the many ways in which the Centre promotes a sense of Irishness.

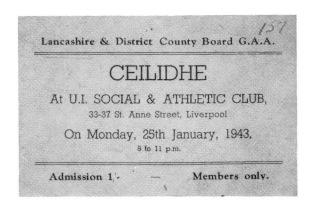

Lancashire & District County Board G.A.A.

CEILIDHE

At U.I. SOCIAL & ATHLETIC CLUB,
33-37 St. Anne Street, Liverpool

On Monday, 25th January, 1943,
8 to 11 p.m.

Admission 1/- — Members only.

"People who never had the remotest interest in the Irish language, even though their background was Irish, came in and when they saw the signs over the toilets saying 'Fir' for men and 'Mna' for women, and 'Oifig' over the office door, and so on and so forth, it reminded them when they were kids that they learnt these things. There was a getting away from the idea that people have in any other country, whether it be England or America or wherever, that if you want to make something look Irish then you paint it green...You didn't see shamrocks, but you saw things like the Claddagh symbol, the St. Brigid's Cross, the Round Tower, things like that. It was more subtle, if you like, and it was carefully thought out. Irish people taking their English friends in had to explain to people the significance of things. Now that in itself made them feel good."

Shay Black, who leads the popular music session at the Centre every Monday night, makes another point:

"It's definitely important that the Irish have some sort of building that is perceived as Irish, without ghettoising people. But you don't need to ghettoise the Irish because the Irish are in all parts of Liverpool society..."

The character and use of the Centre has of course changed over the years as Tommy Walsh points out:

"For the first four or five years of the Irish Centre's opening, it was definitely the Irish community using it, but they brought their friends more. And then there was a period of time when it was very much 'sinn fein'; it was the Irish alone. Nobody else wanted to know them socially ...

"Some people wouldn't go in because they wouldn't want to be associated with the Irish, or others who were afraid to go in because it was a place which was at risk, so the Irish were definitely alone then. I suppose that was for ten years between 1969 and 1979 approximately, and the people began to realise that the 'Troubles' as we saw them in Belfast weren't really mirrored in the Irish community in Liverpool...So there was a sort of broadening of people using the premises for their own social occasions."

The lavish refurbishing of the Centre created a financial crisis which at one stage threatened its survival, until in 1992 local businessman, Michael Finnegan, stepped in to take over ownership. There was some concern that he would change the way the Centre operated, but up until now he has been

11

content to let it continue in much the same way as before. Most people involved with the Centre seem fairly content with the new stewardship, but it is possible that one day the Irish community will again feel the need to own its own Centre and another Irish Centre may emerge.

IRISH TRADITIONAL MUSIC

Traditional music can be defined many ways, but its fundamental characteristic is one of direct transmission. That is, the music is learned from the performances of others, and players of one generation learn from the next in this manner. In the face of global popular music trends, Ireland retains a vigorous, orally transmitted musical tradition.

The national repertoire in Ireland today is rooted in the popular music of Ireland of the Seventeenth and Eighteenth centuries. It consists of instrumental music, mostly dance music, but also songs in Irish and English.

Variation and ornamentation lie at the heart of all traditional playing and singing since it is through variation that technical skill, imaginative powers and personality are expressed. The melody acts only as a skeleton, to which the musicians add flesh.

With regard to the singing; songs in English and songs in the Irish language involve two distinctive vocal styles. The decline of the Irish language made the song tradition vulnerable, but it survived in areas where Irish was still the first spoken language. This form of singing is called the *Sean Nós* style (literally the old style); its defining characteristic is that it is solo unaccompanied singing. It is, then, a pure form of singing which remains oral in its method of transmission.

The English singing style is based on the ballad (a narrative poem or song) particular to English language songs common in both England and America. In effect the Irish adopted the ballad, both lyrically (by the use of Gaelic internal rhymes) and musically. The airs and tunes tended to be based on the rhythms of the dances which were popular.

The most popular dance tunes are jigs and reels, but there also exist hornpipes, polkas, slides and highlands. Although much dance music is now listened to rather than danced to, dancing does still take place, and both England and Ireland are currently in the midst of a major revival of set dancing, encouraged by the G.A.A. (Gaelic Athletic Association) and Comhaltas Ceoltoiri Eireann (The Association of Irish Musicians).

Set dancing is the group dancing of Nineteenth Century Ireland, based mainly on quadrilles (a figure dance of four couples). Each area of the country tended to have its own particular sets and because the set could be got up with groups as small as two couples (the half set), dancing could easily be accommodated in private houses as well as in pubs and other public places. Indeed a great deal of Irish traditional music was played at house parties, at least up until the 1930s when the church, with the aid of the police and the 1936 Irish Public Dance Hall Act, succeeded in finishing off house dances. The priests set up parochial halls to which everyone was expected to go and from which the government collected 25% of the ticket price in tax.

The rise of the dance hall led to the creation of the céilí band. To adapt their music for the dance halls, musicians had to become louder and have a heavier and more rhythmic backing, so the classic line up a céilí band evolved to a fiddle, flute, accordion, piano and drums. (The word **céilí** refers to the practice of gathering in a neighbour's house for chat, story telling, and sometimes dancing.)

The prototype for what became the céilí band first emerged amongst the Irish emigrant groups in England and America at the start of the Twentieth Century, and it was then adopted in the home country.

This parallels the theory of historian Roy Foster, who believes that "Ireland claimed a fiercely and unrealistically obsessive identification from its emigrants."[11] This "obsessive identification" ensured that a musical tradition, long in the doldrums in Ireland, would live to go back home.

Another side to this argument is that colonialism stripped the native Irish of their culture, and music is significant because it was an important way of preserving cultural memory and transmitting it across generations.

The Irish emigrant faces contradictory pressures—on one hand, to become assimilated into the new country, and on the other to affirm exclusive Irishness. Music can play an important role dealing with such pressures as the following quotation from Brid Boland, a woman who left Ireland in the 1980s, shows:

"I know that a lot of people didn't have an interest in Irish music before they left Ireland and they started developing it then. Somehow or other it seems that music goes beyond words, that it is easier to tap into as a way of identifying what your difference is, and it expresses something that is very personal to you. Probably it could be done in other ways, through poetry or art or something, but it seems like music is easier. I think it's part of the whole thing of becoming aware of what being Irish is, which you don't realise until you're placed in a situation which forces you to find out."[12]

14

Comhaltas, or in full, Comhaltas Ceóltoirí Eireann (Association of Irish Musicians), was founded in Ireland in 1951 when traditional music there was in a state of decline and in danger of dying out. To counteract this trend a small group of idealists banded together to form Comhaltas with the aim of promoting Irish traditional music, singing and dancing. Today there are branches in every county in Ireland, thirty-six in Britain, around thirty in the United States, half a dozen in Australia, as well as branches in Sardinia, Tokyo, and Luxembourg.

The Liverpool branch, formed in 1957, is one of the oldest. Two other branches, Glasgow and West London, both strongholds of Irish emigrants, formed at around the same time.

But before Comhaltas was established there were several groups of musicians playing traditional Irish music in Liverpool, at céilís, parties, concerts and dances. Two well known céilí bands were the Shannon Star Band, which played for céilí dancing between the 1940's and the 1970's, and the Brian Boru Céilí Band which was led by Peggy Peakin, now playing in the Liverpool Céilí Band.

Before the opening of Liverpool's Irish Centre, Comhaltas held céilís in places like St Cuthbert's off Prescot Road, St. James and St. Monica's in Bootle, and often in people's houses—a very old tradition in Ireland. Today the Liverpool branch of Comhaltas is one of the biggest in the country, so home-based events are no longer possible.

Sean McNamara, a founding member of Comhaltas and the Liverpool Céilí Band (in which he still plays), remembers the beginnings of the organisation.

"In the early days it was a fairly small, you might say exclusive organisation, because before the Irish Centre opened we used to have our regular meetings in people's houses. So it was almost by invitation, you know. It was a select group who were in the know or who had heard about it. Out of the small group we produced a great band because most of us were musicians or singers. When the Irish Centre opened we were able to expand

15

our activities and the branch grew a lot bigger and we started children's classes. We had great success with teaching young people the music. From that time onwards the young people had far greater opportunities of learning music than we had. As I say we were actually giving people lessons from what was a fairly good standard anyway, whereas before lots of us had to make our own way, learn our own music, and go out and find musicians."

The Liverpool branch is important to the organisation as a whole and Kit Hodge, one of the founding members of the branch, is now Secretary at the Comhaltas Headquarters in Monkstown, Dublin. Mary McAndrew, also heavily involved in the Liverpool branch, is the organisation's secretary for the whole of Britain.

Today Kit Hodge's sister, Peggy Peakin, teaches children how to play the fiddle in the Sunday afternoon sessions in the Irish Centre (she has also been a member of the Liverpool Céilí Band since the late 1960s).

The Comhaltas sessions are considered very important for keeping Irish traditional music alive in Liverpool. For example, many of the people who play at the Monday night sessions at the Irish Centre have come up through Comhaltas. Those who learned to play as children through Comhaltas may

Conn Doyle, Pipe Major, at two Irish Centre teaching sessions in the mid 1960s.

Dancing at an Irish Centre céilí, 1993.

drop out when they leave school, go to college, or get married, but some return to the fold when they are older or send their own children. Two Liverpool based Irish bands, Geraldine and the Three Counties and Blackbush, contain members of Comhaltas classes.

A concert given by Comhaltas one Sunday afternoon in March 1993 gave a very clear demonstration of the overall strength of the organisation when the Senior and Junior Grúpa Ceoil (music group) ran through their competition pieces. A Grúpa Ceoil can have up to twenty members, with the ages in these groups ranging from around seven to seventy. The main hall in the Irish Centre was packed with family and friends showing their interest and support of the musical activities.

Michael Coyne, a Bootle-born semi-professional musician, remembers going to the Irish Centre on Sundays to learn how to play at the Comhaltas sessions.

"Well, first you started learning the tin whistle. It was the lightest thing any one of six (years) could hold. You couldn't carry much else. Then you kind of moved around to the violin or fiddle, and then the accordion (which

17

he plays now) from about 12 I'd say. When I was first going (about 1969/70) there was nowhere else to learn Irish music.

"At the time, I suppose I felt I was pushed into it. You didn't want to come in and have to practice. When I was first learning the accordion, Sean Murphy used to teach us. He was a member of the Liverpool Céilí Band. He'd be able to say right away, 'You haven't practiced this week' because you wouldn't know the tune.

"As you moved up we got a bit split up. Like the girls went off and got married or whatever. The 16-18 céilí band was the last one that we were all really involved in and lots of them kind of left because they were out with fellas or whatever".

The Liverpool Céilí Band at the Irish Centre in the mid 1960s.

Today there are a number of traditional Irish groups active in the Liverpool area, such as Finn's Hotel and The Carlin Céilí Band, but The Liverpool Céilí Band are probably still the most well known.

The Liverpool Céilí Band grew out of the early days of Comhaltas and was formed to enter competitions and festivals in Ireland. Its members have included Sean McNamara, Eamon Coyne, and Kit Hodge.

The name of the Liverpool Céilí Band is still renowned wherever traditional Irish music is played because the band twice (1963 and 1964) won the All Ireland competition. Sean McNamara offers one explanation of why the band were so successful:

"Well, we were playing so often was one side of it. Enthusiasm. And as much as anything else we were a real well-practiced céilí band because we were playing so often.

"We used to play regularly at St. Mary's in Highfield Street on Sunday nights and at St Cuthbert's off Prescot Road. At the time we competed, because we were playing so often at céilís, we had a great swing and rhythm which I suppose helped us to win. We always played as if for a hall full of dancers, because that was what we were used to. Liverpool has a great reputation in traditional music through the Céilí Band but also through the achievements of the youngsters. They do expect, when it comes to traditional music, a high standard from anyone that comes out of Liverpool."

The Céilí Band made two records on the Rex label (a subsidiary of Decca): 'Champions Twice' (1965) and 'We're Off To Dublin' (1966).

The Liverpool Céilí Band still plays today, although Sean McNamara is the only original member involved. Eamon Coyne, the other main stalwart of the band, died in 1990 but his sons, Terry and Eamon, now play in the band, thus continuing the family tradition. Kevin Webster, whose father was a member over a decade ago, also plays in the band, and Peggy Peakin, sister of another original member Kit Hodge, has been in the band since 1965.

The band are still very much in demand, with a regular monthly booking at the Irish Centre which attracts large audiences of all ages, and almost everybody joins in with the dancing. Today there are other Irish bands in Liverpool playing traditional music and a mixture of traditional/country and western.

Since the death of Eamon Coyne, the Céilí Band have not been on what used to be regular trips to Ireland, but whenever any of these musicians get together tales of those trips come flooding out. Liverpool's Irish musicians always seem to place great store in playing in the "home" country, and the trips are remembered as being great fun, as Terry Coyne recalls...

"The band always consisted of about 15 members by the time we got over there, about eight from here and we picked up seven while we were over there. Most nights we ended up with about thirty people on stage sitting around, playing music. The actual situation, when you do go over, is you all meet up with the people that you've known and you'll go out and you'll find a pub and you'll play all day and you'll love it."

Visiting Ireland is one very visible way in which Irish identity is expressed, and the trips to Ireland organised by P.J. McCarthy, the Irish-

Neil Lynch, Theresa Lynch and Sibohán Morrison learning to play the piano accordion at a Comhaltas session. (photo. D. Massey).

The Liverpool Céilí Band today. (photo. D. Massey).

born singer with Cream of the Barley (the leading Irish pub band in the city) emphasises the strength of the links between Liverpool and Ireland and the importance people place on this link.

"We used to have a great time years ago when the boat went from Liverpool. We'd do these trips to Dublin and there would be 200 or so of us going and it would be unbelievable. We had some great days there and there's some unbelievable stories. We brought extra people back with us, we lost people, all sorts of things.

"We used to play on the boat. The first time we ever went there were 200 of us in the bar which was only meant to hold 150. We were going to play all night and we had different people with us who were going to get up. We decided we'd start playing when the boat left and begin with 'The Leaving of Liverpool' just to be really on the ball.

"The boat was due to leave at ten o'clock and at about quarter past it starts vibrating and we thought it was going so we started singing. We finished off at about 11.15 and looked out and we hadn't even moved. We were knackered and we hadn't even started!"

21

Musician Brid Boland expresses an alternative view about the value of returning to Ireland:

"I go back every year, to go to music festivals and listen to a lot of music, and I am replenished, renourished through it in a way that going anywhere else on holiday wouldn't do...couldn't do."[13]

Members of the Maírin Bolger Dancing School at the Irish Centre. (photo. D. Massey).

TUNES AND PINTS: LIVERPOOL SESSIONS

In Liverpool, a good deal of traditional Irish music-making takes place in a fairly informal setting, which generally goes under the name of a "session."

For people expecting the usual "stage/band/audience" format, the session is a surprise. Players play together, for each other, with an intrinsic part of the tradition being that there is no audience in the usual sense, rather an extended group with musicians and listeners alike included in the music-making.

Liverpool musician Eamon Coyne gives an impression of how a session works: "It doesn't matter where you go (in Ireland), you can walk into a pub where there's some musicians playing, and you can walk straight in, not knowing them, and within five minutes they'll be buying you a pint and you'll be playing tunes with them. That's the good thing about it. That's the thing with trad; it's very social."

The most well attended traditional Irish music session in Liverpool today takes place every Monday night at the Irish Centre. The large numbers attending this session, give an indication of the strength of traditional Irish music in the city.

The session is led by the Irish-born Shay Black who was asked to start it off (along with three other local musicians) when the centre was refurbished. Since then the session has gone from strength to strength, and as Shay argues:

"You could actually say there's been a bit of a rejuvenation of traditional music and session music in Liverpool. We've been encouraged to stay here and there's times when you feel it hasn't been too good, mainly because it's been too popular. When it's too popular the musicians can't hear each other. But we've managed to control this. I mean, Irish music is basically dance music so you're bound to have noise around it of people talking and dancing and having a good time. But dance music hides virtuoso performances on individual instruments that you can't usually hear in the conglomerate that is a session. So as well as asking people to be quiet during singing performances, I will occasionally ask people to be quiet during performances on instruments."

23

A traditional music session at the Irish Centre. (photo. D. Massey).

Incidentally Shay, along with a few other musicians from the session, is also a member of the well respected traditional Irish music group Garva.

Alan Barnat, a Midlands-born musician who has lived in Liverpool for almost twenty years, describes how he sees the session at the Irish Centre working:

"There are a group of four or five of them who are like regular leaders of the session. Probably most people who play or sing Irish music in Liverpool go down at some stage or another. It's not brilliant, but it's good in the sense that you meet lots of people and you're playing lots of different tunes. It's not a brilliant place to play in because it's so big and the acoustics are very difficult, especially when there's lots of people in there talking or whatever.

"It works like a normal session in that theoretically anyone starts a tune and the others join in. In fact it's a bit hard because of the acoustics in there, so you can't always hear people. So the people with the loudest instruments and the ones that are organising the session tend to start it off a lot. Shay sort of MC's it, which mainly means calling for singers and keeping people quiet.

"When there's a visiting musician or anyone who's particularly good, he tries to get them to play a tune so that people can listen to them."

Terry Coyne, a regular at the Irish Centre session, goes some way to explaining why musicians enjoy these gatherings: "The whole crack of the session and most traditional music is not just about tunes or even the songs. It's the whole package. The performance is just a little part of it. If you're looking forward to playing music you usually play to your best. Then when the drink sets in the jokes start, and the songs come out and the stories start. The quickest way to become an alcoholic is to become an Irish musician because it just goes along with it."

Kevin Webster (another Irish Centre session regular) compares playing Irish music in pub bands, to playing traditional music in sessions, and he draws out the attraction of the latter.

"One of them is unsocial and one is totally social and that's ours. One of them you're totally separate from the people you're playing for and the other one you're playing with people and the people around you are part of it. You have the crack and nobody cares. You just play."

This quote brings out an important point about the audience-performer relationship at a session. As already noted, at a session there is no real audience because it is a participative event and everyone is involved. The people in the pub, or the room, are as much a part of the occasion as the musicians or singers, and generally anybody is at liberty to contribute a song or a tune. Musicians are free to get up, in mid-tune if they wish, go to the bar, chat to people, and begin playing again when they feel like it. The noise and the atmosphere generated by the non-musicians is an important part of the event, and there is no real sense that performers and non- musicians are separated.

Kevin Webster makes a point about the importance of the Irish Centre session: "The good thing about this session, when it started, was that all the people who had been secretly practising and learning the music started coming down, which wasn't happening before because nothing was going on in Liverpool. When these people started hearing about the session then they thought, 'Well we'll go out and play.' Now it's brought a lot more people out who were secretly playing at home, listening to tapes, and who had nowhere to play.

"There's an awful lot of students here learning the instruments and there's about fifteen of them coming in on Monday nights playing away, which is great. We've actually got several students who are class musicians choosing to come to Liverpool because they know they'll be around a few good musicians."

Outside of the Irish Centre the sessions in Liverpool are now thin on the ground. This situation compares rather unfavourably with that in Manchester, where sessions take place virtually every night in a number of venues. The Irish-born community in that city is much bigger and younger than in Liverpool and there are probably also more Irish landlords. Young Irish people go there to study and to find work (which is more plentiful than in Liverpool) and they are also taking part in sessions.

Sean McNamara describes the situation that existed in Liverpool in the 1940s, when he was in his twenties.

"There was far less of a culture for going out to the pub then. Certainly there weren't sessions. If we had sessions at all it was in people's houses. But there wasn't a lot of it. There's far more music in pubs now than there ever used to be. At one time you wouldn't be allowed to play or sing a song

Shay Black, one of the leaders of the Irish Centre session. (photo. D. Massey).

26

in a pub. It's a more recent development. Later on there were sessions here over the years, but not many. There wouldn't be more than one a week. I remember there used to be a great session in The Cracke, and there used to be one in Peter Kavanagh's years ago. The thing was that when there was a session on somewhere that was the only place that was on at the time, and then a few months later it would move on to somewhere else."

McNamara also has a very plausible explanation of why there have been fewer sessions here than in London and Manchester.

"Maybe in these places (London and Manchester) there would be a lot of Irish men who came over here to work and who were musicians. So when they went out for a drink they would want to play music as well. Whereas in Liverpool we didn't seem to have that. Most people playing music here tended to be Liverpudlians of Irish descent, so they had their homes and their houses, whereas other people would live in digs and go out to the pub to meet their work mates and didn't have the same sort of settlement."

There are a variety of other reasons why the number of sessions in Liverpool has declined over the years. One of them, cited by a number of people, is that key players in a session often move on and leave the city altogether. In Liverpool, with the decline of employment opportunities, this is particularly pertinent.

In addition, there is the problem of finding pub landlords willing to let a session take place. In the past in Liverpool this would have proved difficult because of the history of sectarian strife and the stereotype of the drunken Irishman likely to get into a fight. "Singing was seen as trouble," in any case, as Stan Ambrose recalls, and it is easy to imagine a situation where a Protestant man singing an Orange song could provoke an incident with Catholic men in the pub and vice versa, so landlords would be wary of allowing potentially provocative Irish music in their pub.

Ambrose, a folk musician and presenter of a folk music show on local radio, remembers a session at a pub called The Victoria in St John's Lane in the early 1960s.

"The Victoria was the centre of folk activity in Liverpool. There used to be two sessions in there. In one room there was a singing room which was strictly traditional and you daren't bring an instrument in there. In the other

A typical Monday night at the Irish Centre, 1994. (photo. D. Massey).

part of the bar was the beginnings of people bringing in instruments to play. We formed a little band called Mabel's Céilí Band and we played Irish music. We mixed an Orange song with a Green song in the same session. Sectarianism was out the window then. It was a very limited repertoire but it was Irish."

Following this period, Stan singles out a session which took place at the Irish Centre on Sunday afternoons in the mid-1960s.

"A lot of young people, who are now not so young, used to come down and that's where they started getting involved, that's how groups started to form. They used to go out and start sessions in pubs. So there was The Cracke and The Belvedere and the Irish Centre.

"I suppose the reasons sessions die out in particular places is because they get too packed or sometimes people move on. One reason why there aren't so many sessions now is just that it's difficult to find pubs that will let you.

"There used to be a law in Liverpool about playing instruments in pubs and we used to have to be very careful. That's why we had these singarounds. I think managers of pubs were always very concerned about music because singing was seen as trouble."

Shay Black got involved in sessions in Liverpool more or less by accident after stumbling across a folk club called Oily Joe's in a Dock Road pub.

"Then we used to have sessions very similar to the ones we have now in the Irish Centre in a place called The Cracke. I sang there with a couple called Mick and Elaine Johnson, and a brother of Terry Coyne, young Mick Coyne, who was a piper."

Alan Barnat, who goes to the Irish Centre session, describes how he got involved in sessions led by Mick Johnson at The Belvedere pub:

"When I first came here (in 1976) I didn't know anybody so I used to go to a session. There was a regular Tuesday night session in The Belvedere pub. I bought a tin whistle and I knew a few of the tunes so I just joined in occasionally. There was probably about ten or twelve musicians but the rest of the room was packed out.

"That session lasted about two or three years and after The Belvedere finished there was another big session every Sunday afternoon in The Cracke which went on for a long time. That involved people like young Eamon Coyne; Terry, his brother; Tony Gibbons; and Keith Price. I think that session went on for years until we got moved out of there. The session moved to a little pub on the Dock Road which lasted for a few years.

"Then a piper called Phil Westwell started off a session in about 1984/5, which was at the Newstead Abbey (on Smithdown Road) most of the time. That lasted for about five years until he left Liverpool a couple of years ago."

P.J. McCarthy from Cream of the Barley started off a session a few years ago in a pub called Patrick's (also known as The Dart) and this served to inspire other musicians.

"The great thing about it was that it became very successful in the sense that we got very few musicians who were playing, but we got a lot of fellas who wanted to play, and a lot of fellas who got the confidence to play. The strange thing is that out of that session there's about five bands now on the road with fellas who started off in there. It gave them the confidence and it gave them the chance to practice and build up a little bit of a repertoire."

This underlines the importance of sessions in invigorating the musical life of the city, and while sessions continue to exist in Liverpool it is likely that the Irish music scene in the city will continue to remain healthy.

I've got Irish bands booked now for the next twelve months—they just draw the customers in. (Tom Carr, owner of The Easby pub, quoted in *The Liverpool Echo* 11.12.92)

Many of the musicians who went to the session with P. J. McCarthy at The Dart eventually ended up in bands playing Irish music around the pubs of Liverpool. Irish music in the pubs is a relatively recent phenomenon, beginning in 1984 when a local businessman, Bob Burns, opened a pub in Mathew Street called Flanagan's Apple. Now, in 1994, you can hear a band playing Irish music in an Irish-style Liverpool city centre pub any night of the week. The names of the pubs (Flanagan's, Guinan's, Kitty O'Shea's, Rosie O'Grady's) and the bands (Cream of the Barley, Black Velvet, The Hooleys, Blarney Stone) leave little doubt as to what to expect from these establishments.

The same (or similar) pub names can be found across the world, in cities such as New York, Boston, Sydney, even Prague, where Irish expatriates and Irish music fans gather.

In many ways these popular pubs have transformed nights out in Liverpool city centre for many people. Everyone now knows where Flanagan's is and what goes on there, but this wasn't always the case, as McCarthy from Cream of the Barley, explains:

"In the beginning you couldn't explain to anyone where Flanagan's was. Now you could tell them where the town hall is from Flanagan's."

Cream of the Barley are in fact central to the whole story of the boom in Irish pub music in Liverpool, although their involvement came about quite accidentally, as McCarthy recounts:

"We used to go out drinking every Sunday and someone said to us that there was a new Irish pub that we should go and see. That was Flanagan's. We came down about noon, but it was all boarded up with these metal shutters, so we went for a few drinks elsewhere and played a bit of music. About half past three we went to the John Lennon bar in Mathew Street

Cream of the Barley on stage at Guinan's.

because that was generally open. There was no one in there so we just started playing and eventually it filled up.

"We were there until seven o'clock and as we came out we were opposite Flanagan's so we thought, seeing as that was what we'd come for, we'd best go in and see what was going on. I had a bodhrán (a traditional Irish hand drum), Eddie had a banjo and mandolin, and John had his guitar. As we went in the door Eddie fell in—that was our introduction to Flanagan's!

"There was only two people in there—Bob Burns (the owner) and Joan Knibb (the manageress). Then the fella from the John Lennon bar came in and he told them that we'd put on a great show. Joan came over and asked if we were a band and when I said that we were she asked if we could come and play on the Wednesday, which was the official opening. So we did and then we played the next Wednesday and so on.

"We were there for about three months, getting odd little audiences, but very little really. We didn't have any gear or anything. But what really made it work was a show of faith and genius on Joan's part. She said come and do Sunday night as well, whereas anybody else would have said go home altogether. "So we started doing Sunday nights downstairs and all of a sudden it started to fill up because people who came on Sundays started coming on Wednesdays as well. And all of a sudden you couldn't bloody move down there. Then, like anything else that's successful, people from other pubs came in and thought they'd have a go. At one time at our peak we were doing nine bookings a week."

Today there is music seven nights a week at Flanagan's, and the pub has even expanded, opening a third floor four or five years ago. The Flanagan's formula proved so popular that owner Bob Burns has opened four more pubs (Guinan's, Rosie O'Grady's, Kitty O'Shea's and the Slaughterhouse) in the last few years.

There are a number of reasons why the Irish pub scene has taken off so quickly and in such a big way in Liverpool. Nuala O'Connor, in *Bringing It All Back Home*, cites the success in the 1980s of bands like The Pogues, The Waterboys, and Van Morrison who all brought Irish music to young mass audiences (although in the case of Cream of the Barley, they are in fact closer to groups like The Dubliners and The Clancys than to The Pogues).

"The Pogues and Shane MacGowan took traditional and folk-based Irish music and fired it in the crucible of modern Irish emigration....they played a chaotic set of stock Irish rebel tunes in London clubs. Pogues music represented children of the Sixties born after Carlow building workers had set up home with Mayo nurses. They rejected the anodyne ballad culture their parents identified with. The Pogues showed a way in which they could be Irish in Britain. The music was exciting and contemporary in form and culture, yet it was culturally familiar also."[14]

This may have applied in Liverpool, where many people in their twenties and thirties may well have been aware of their Irish background but perhaps could not see how music like the traditional music at the Irish Centre had any relevance to them. By the time Flanagan's came along many young people were quite happy to stand there proclaiming their Irish roots and singing along to 'Whisky In The Jar'.

Today, St. Patrick's night is probably celebrated with just as much vigour in Liverpool as it is in Dublin. Flanagan's and the other Irish pubs are packed from early evening. For one night it suddenly seems as though everybody in Liverpool is Irish and proud of it.

Elvis Costello (who was himself born into the Irish community of Birkenhead) has described The Pogues music as "a promise of a good time", and this certainly holds true for Irish pub music in Liverpool. On any night of the week Flanagans is usually full, with an audience made up of people of all ages, but with the majority in their twenties and thirties. There is usually a lively, informal atmosphere with people shouting out requests, joining in with the songs, and sometimes dancing.

Most bands playing in Flanagans will typically include in their repertoire songs such as "Leaving of Liverpool," "Wild Rover," "Whisky In The Jar," "Black Velvet Band," and "Seven Drunken Nights."

Cream of the Barley's PJ McCarthy makes an interesting point about the band's material.

"A lot of the material we play is almost indigenous because with a lot of the songs people just know them and they don't even know why they know them. They don't even know where they heard them—they've just been around that long. They've been brought up in that environment where someone else was singing when they were a kid and you get people going 'Oh I know that song,' although they've never learnt it. They've never bought a record with it on, they just know it."

Paddy Wack at Kitty O'Shea's.

34

P.J. McCarthy also has some interesting points to make regarding the choice of material and sectarianism, which indicate that even though outright religious conflict died out a long time ago in the city, people are still aware of this divide, perhaps because of the proximity of 'the troubles' in Belfast.

"We often get asked for rebel songs and I know some great rebel songs, but I wouldn't sing them. Not because of the politics of them or that, I wouldn't be part of that, but it's just that for every political song that you sing you'd need to be there all night to explain what it was about, and even then a lot of people might miss the point anyway. If people want to take offence, they're not going to listen to what you've got to say about it anyway. The easiest way is just not to do it, and the thing is there's plenty of good songs which won't offend anyone."

On a related theme, Gerry Smyth, a musician who used to play the Irish pubs in Liverpool, looked at the different "versions" of Irishness being evoked by people and songs in the bars.[15] He described an evening playing in one of these pubs and explained why he turned down requests to perform two particular songs. The first request was made by a young man who, after his request for "A Nation Once Again" was turned down, retorted with the line "You're not fucking Irish at all." (Smyth characterised this person as typically being second- or third-generation Irish, easily able to reconcile the pseudo-Irish and English elements in his life.)

The second request was for 'The Birmingham Six' by The Pogues which, when turned down, was met with a disgruntled "You haven't a clue, have you."

Smyth explains his refusal of these requests:

"It was not playing 'A Nation Once Again' to which I objected that night. It was the ethos which evocation in that situation implied, and the idea of nationhood on which it traded. As far as I was concerned the ex-pat must be made to signify something different from the old stereotype."[16]

Smyth goes on to explain why he turned down the request for "The Birmingham Six."

"It seemed too easy an option in the pub as a means of parading our dissent, a mere carnival ride that could be turned off with the lights at the end of the evening."[17]

When this musician attempted to break out of the available roles and offer a less familiar form of Irishness, the audience were completely unresponsive. He eventually accepted the inevitable and presented the audience with the sort of Irishness they wanted in the shape of songs like "Whisky In the Jar" and "Seven Drunken Nights."

In a survey carried out in Liverpool in 1988, Elizabeth Ives asked the respondents (a mixture of first-, second- and third-generation Irish) how they ranked in importance various cultural activities to Irish national identity.[18] She found that Irish music and dance were seen as the most important, followed by Catholic religion, although she admits that, to some extent the ordering of the attributes reflects "exportability" and the priorities of popular culture.

"Irish music (via Comhaltas, the radio, and on records or cassettes), dance (via the Irish Centre) and religious institutions are more accessible to the Irish in Liverpool, as well as being of importance to national self image in Ireland, than are Irish books or the occasion to use the Irish language."[19]

Liverpool may no longer be able to lay claim to the title "the capital of Ireland," but the recent boom in Irish pub music demonstrates the strength of the latent "Irishness" that exists in the city. It is an Irishness so deeply engrained in the history of the city that it is never likely to disappear.

A busy time at Flanagan's—the scene on St. Patrick's night.

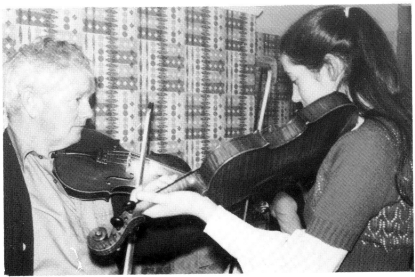

Ensuring that the music lives on: Peggy Peakin and the late Eamon Coyne instructing young students.

NOTES AND REFERENCES

1. Lennon, Mary et al, *Across The Water. Irish Women's Lives in Britain.* Virago, 1988. p.74.

2. Neal, Frank, *Sectarian Violence. The Liverpool Experience 1819 - 1914.* Manchester University Press, 1988. p.7.

3. Ibid p.82.

4. Swift, R. and Gilley, S. (eds), *The Irish In Britain 1815 - 1939.* Pinter, 1989. p.104.

5. Davis, Graham, *The Irish In Britain 1815 - 1914.* Gill and Macmillan, Dublin, 1991. p.120.

6. *Report on the state of the Irish Poor in Great Britain (1836).* Appendix II. pp.19-20.

7. Neal, op cit. p.185.

8. O'Mara, Pat, *Autobiography of a Liverpool Irish Slummy.* Hopkinson, 1934. p.10.

9. Ibid.

10. Ayers, Pat, *The Liverpool Docklands. Life and Work In Athol Street.* Docklands History Project, 1990. p.159.

11. O'Connor, Nuala, *Bringing It All Back Home.* BBC Books, 1991, p.62.

12. Lennon, op cit. p.72.

13. Lennon, op cit. p.74.

14. O'Connor, op cit. p.158.

15. Smyth, Gerry, *Who's The Greenest Of Them All? Irishness and Popular Music.* Irish Studies Review No. 2, Winter 1992. pp.3-5.

16. Ibid.

17. Ibid.

18. Ives, Elizabeth, *The Irish in Liverpool. A Study of Ethnic Identification and Social Participation.* Unpublished MA Thesis, University of Liverpool 1988.

19. Ibid, p.299.

Liverpool Sounds Series

Céilís, Jigs and Ballads: Irish Music In Liverpool

Nashville of the North: Country Music In Liverpool

Harmonious Relations: Popular Music in Family Life on Merseyside

Forthcoming:

Dance Bands of the '30s & '40s

Music of the Black Communities of Liverpool

Liverpool Rock Music of the '70s & '80s

The Leverhulme Research Team:

Sara Cohen

Kevin McManus

Tricia Jenkins

Connie Atkinson

Derek Murray

To order, send £3.95 plus £2 p&p to

Institute of Popular Music

Box 147 University of Liverpool

Liverpool L69 3BX